THE NEW BEST OF

THE Beach Boys

Project Manager: Jeannette DeLisa

© 1996 WARNER BROS. PUBLICATIONS
All Rights Reserved

CONTENTS

GOOD VIBRATIONS

Words and Music by
BRIAN WILSON and
MIKE LOVE

Good Vibrations - 3 - 1

4

CHORUS

Good Vibrations - 3 - 2

Good Vibrations - 3 - 3

BARBARA ANN

Words and Music by
FRED FASSERT

Barbara Ann - 2 - 1

CALIFORNIA GIRLS

Words and Music by
BRIAN WILSON

California Girls - 2 - 1

WOULDN'T IT BE NICE?

Words by
BRIAN WILSON and TONY ASHER

Music by
BRIAN WILSON

Would-n't it be nice if we were old - er__ Then__ we would-n't have to wait__ so__
nice if we could wake__ up__ In__ the morn-ing when the day__ is__

long____ And would-n't it be nice to live to-ge - ther In__ the kind of
new____ And af - ter that to spend the day to-ge - ther Hold__ each oth - er

world where we'd__ be - long____ Though it's gon-na make it that much bet - ter__
close the whole__ night__ through__ The hap - py times to-geth - er we'd been spend-ing__

When we can say good-night and stay to-geth - er__ Would-n't it be
I wish that ev - 'ry kiss was nev - er end - ing__

Wouldn't It Be Nice? - 2 - 1

Wouldn't It Be Nice? - 2 - 2

SURFER GIRL

Words and Music by
BRIAN WILSON

Slow Rock beat

Lit - tle surf - er, lit - tle one, made my heart come all un - done. Do you love me,

do you, surf - er girl? I have watched you on the shore,

stand - ing by the o - cean's roar. Do you love me, do you, surf - er girl?

Surfer Girl - 2 - 1

FUN, FUN, FUN

Words and Music by
BRIAN WILSON and MICHAEL LOVE

Bright Rock-Boogie beat

1. Well, she got her dad-dy's car and she cruised through the ham-burg-er stand_
girls can't stand her 'cause she walks, looks and drives like an ace_

_ now.___
_ now.___

Seems she for-got all a-bout_ the li-
She makes the "In-dy" five hun-dred look

Fun, Fun, Fun - 4 - 1

brar - y like she told her "Old man"__ now._____
like a Ro - man char - i - ot race__ now._____

And with her
A lot - ta

ra - di - o blast - in', goes cruis - in' just as fast as she can __ now. _____
guys try to catch __ her, but she leads 'em on a wild goose chase __ now. _____ }

And she'll have fun, fun, fun, till her dad - dy takes the T - Bird a - way.__

1. D   2. D

2. Well,   the

16

A-well, you knew all a-long____ that your dad was get-tin' wise to you____ now.____ And since he took your set of keys you've been think-in' that your fun is all through_ now.____ But you can

Fun, Fun, Fun - 4 - 4

I GET AROUND

Words and Music by
BRIAN WILSON

I Get Around - 2 - 1

LITTLE DEUCE COUPE

Words by
ROGER CHRISTIAN

Music by
BRIAN WILSON

Little Deuce Coupe - 4 - 1

Little Deuce Coupe - 4 - 2

Little Deuce Coupe - 4 - 4

WILD HONEY

Words and Music by
BRIAN WILSON and
MICHAEL LOVE

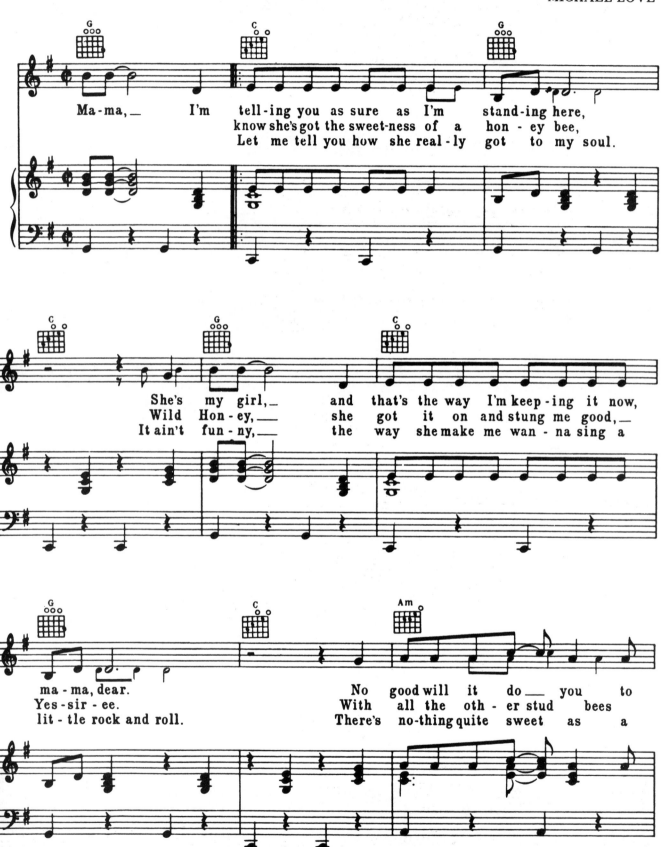

25

Wild Honey - 2 - 2

SURFER'S RULE

Words and Music by
BRIAN WILSON and
MICHAEL LOVE

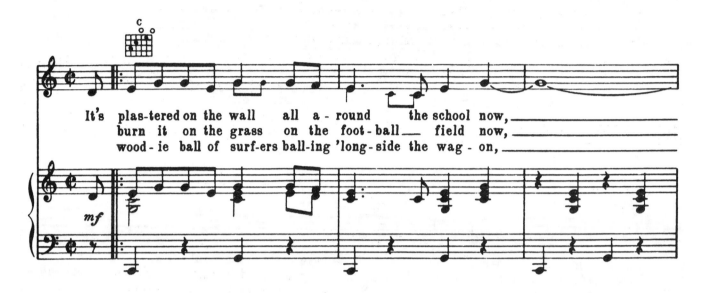

It's plas-tered on the wall all a - round the school now, ___
burn it on the grass on the foot-ball field now, ___
wood - ie ball of surf-ers ball-ing 'long-side the wag - on, ___

Be - com-ing just as com-mon as the Gold - en Rule now. ___
Just try to make them cool it and they'll nev - er yield now. ___
The hoe - dad-dies sit-tin' while the surf-ers are drag - gin'. ___

Take it ___ or leave it, ___ But you
Take what ___ you've heard now, ___ And ___
The surf - ers ___ are win - ning, ___ And they

Surfer's Rule - 2 - 1

LITTLE HONDA

Words and Music by
BRIAN WILSON and
MICHAEL LOVE

Bright Rock beat

Litte Honda - 2 - 1

Put on a rag-ged sweat-shirt, I'll take you an-y-where you want me to.___
We'll ride on out-a the town to an-y-place I know you like.___
I bet-ter turn on the light so we can ride my Hon-da to-night.___

First gear, it's all right;___ sec-ond gear,___

a-lean right;___ third gear,___ hang on tight.___

Fast-er,___ it's all right. It's not a right. It climbs the right. First

1. 2. 3. D. S. 𝄋 and fade

DO IT AGAIN

Words and Music by
BRIAN WILSON and MICHAEL LOVE

Do It Again - 2 - 1

Do It Again - 2 - 2

IN MY ROOM

Words and Music by
BRIAN WILSON and GARY USHER

33

In My Room - 2 - 2

THE WARMTH OF THE SUN

Words and Music by
BRIAN WILSON and
MICHAEL LOVE

The Warmth Of The Sun - 3 - 1

The Warmth Of The Sun - 3 - 2

36

like she's still theirs _____ the way that I feel. _____

My love's like the warmth_ of the sun, it won't ev - er

Repeat and fade

die. _____ Ooh. _____

Repeat and fade

The Warmth Of The Sun - 3 - 3

DON'T WORRY BABY

Words by
BRIAN WILSON, ROGER CHRISTIAN,
JAY SIEGEL, PHILIP MARGO,
HENRY MEDRESS and MITCHELL MARGO

Music by
BRIAN WILSON and ROGER CHRISTIAN

Don't Worry Baby - 3 - 1

Don't Worry Baby - 3 - 3

SURFIN' SAFARI

Words and Music by
BRIAN WILSON and
MICHAEL LOVE

Surfin' Safari - 3 - 1

42

In Hunt - ing - ton and Ma - li - bu they're

shoot - in' the pier, __ In Rin - con, they're walk - in' the nose. __

We're go - in' on sa - fa - ri to the is - lands this year, __ so if you're

com - in', get read - y to go. __ They're __

Surfin' Safari - 3 - 3

SHUT DOWN

Words by
ROGER CHRISTIAN

Music by
BRIAN WILSON

Shut Down - 3 - 1

out in low,— but my fuel - in - ject - ed Sting-ray's real - ly start - in' to go. To

get the trac - tion I'm rid - in' the clutch;— my pres-sure plate is burn - in'; that ma - chin's too much.—

D. S. 𝄋 al Coda

Coda

Repeat and fade

Shut it off, shut it off,

Repeat and fade

bud - dy, now I shut you down.—

ALL SUMMER LONG

Words and Music by
BRIAN WILSON

Sit - tin' in my car out - side your house, ___
Minia - ture golf and hunt - in' in the hills, ___

Re - mem - ber when you spilled coke all o - ver your
When we rode that horse we ___ got ___ a

blouse; ___
thrill; ___

Tee shirts, cut - offs, and a pair of
Ev - 'ry now and then we hear our

All Summer Long - 2 - 1

CATCH A WAVE

Words and Music by
BRIAN WILSON

GIRLS ON THE BEACH

Words and Music by
BRIAN WILSON and
MICHAEL LOVE

Girls On The Beach - 2 - 1

WENDY

Words and Music by
BRIAN WILSON

Wen - dy,__ Wen - dy, what went wrong?__ Oh so
Wen - dy,__ Wendy, don't lose your head,__ Lose your
Wen - dy,__ I wouldn't hurt you like that,__ No, no,

wrong. We went__ to-ge-ther for so long.__
head. Wen - dy,__ don't believe a word he said.__
no. I thought we had our love down pat.

Wendy - 2 - 1

PLEASE LET ME WONDER

Words and Music by
BRIAN WILSON and
MICHAEL LOVE

Moderately

Now,_ here we are to - geth - er,   this would -'ve been worth wait - ing for - ev - er;
I built_ all   my goals a - round_ you   that some - day my love would sur - round you;

I_ al - ways knew it's feel this way._____
you'll_ nev - er know what we've been through._____

Please Let Me Wonder - 2 - 1

DANCE, DANCE, DANCE

Words and Music by
BRIAN WILSON and CARL WILSON

Dance, Dance, Dance - 2 - 1

Dance, Dance, Dance - 2 - 2

PET SOUNDS

By
BRIAN WILSON

HELP ME RHONDA

Words and Music by
BRIAN WILSON

Medium rock

VERSE

1. Since she put me down I've been out doin' in my head,—
2. gon-na be my wife and I was gon-na be her man,—

Come in late at night and in the
But she let an-oth-er guy come be-

morn-in' I just lay in bed;— Well,
tween us and it ruined our plans;— Well,

Rhon-da you look so fine, And I know it would-n't take much time, For you to
Rhon-da you caught my eye,— And I'll give you lots of rea-sons why,— You got-ta

Help Me Rhonda - 3 - 1

help me, Rhon-da, Help me get her out of my heart.___

CHORUS

Help me, Rhon - da! Help, Help me, Rhon - da! Help me, Rhon - da!

Help, Help me, Rhon - da! Help me, Rhon - da! Help, Help me, Rhon - da!

Help me, Rhon - da! Help, Help me, Rhon - da! Help me, Rhon - da!

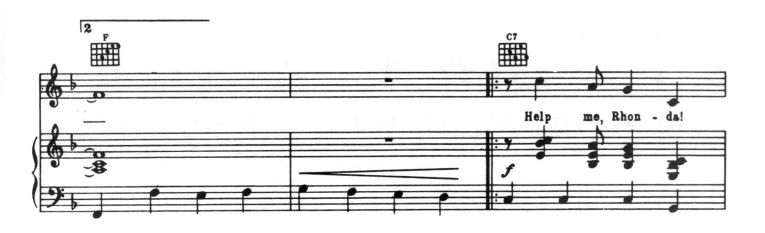

Help Me Rhonda - 3 - 3

YOU'RE SO GOOD TO ME

Words and Music by
BRIAN WILSON

1. You're _ kin - da small and you're _ such a doll, I'm glad _ you're mine _____
2. _ take my hand and you _ un - der-stand when I _____ get in a bad _____
3. _ know your eyes are not _ on the guys, when we're _ a - part _____
4. _ ev - 'ry night you hold _ me so tight when I _____ kiss you _____ good-

_ You're so good _ to me _____ How come you _ are _____
mood, You're so good _ to me _____ How come you _ are _____
_ You're so true _ to me _____ How come you _ are _____
bye, You're so good _ to me _____

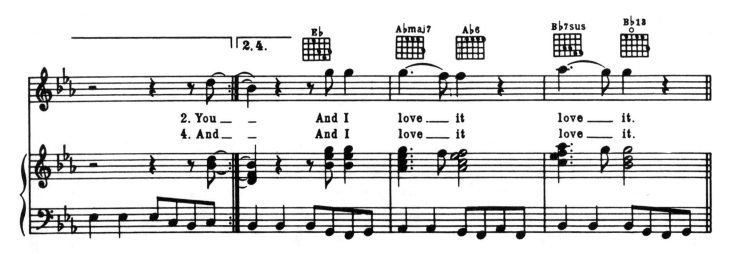

2. You _ _ And I love _ it love _ it.
4. And _ _ And I love _ it love _ it.

You're So Good To Me - 2 - 1

You're So Good To Me - 2 - 2

409

Words and Music by
BRIAN WILSON and GARY USHER

WHEN I GROW UP
(To Be A Man)

Words and Music by
BRIAN WILSON

When I grow up___ to be a man.

Will I dig the same_ things that turn me on as a kid?___
look for the same_ things in a wom-an that I did in a girl?___
kids be proud or think their old man is real-ly a square?___

Will I look back and say_ that I wish I had-n't done what I did?_
Will I set-tle down fast or will I first wan-na trav-el the world?_
When they're out hav-in' fun_ yea, will I still wan-na have my share?

When I Grow Up - 3 - 1

SURFIN' U.S.A.

Lyric by
BRIAN WILSON

Music by
CHUCK BERRY

Surfin' U.S.A. - 2 - 1